10746
9 E.13541 KAT

P9-DNK-361

Great Country Walks Around Toronto

–within reach by public transit

Elliott Katz
Illustrated by Leong Leung

THE ONTARIO HISTORICAL SOCIETY

Great North Books

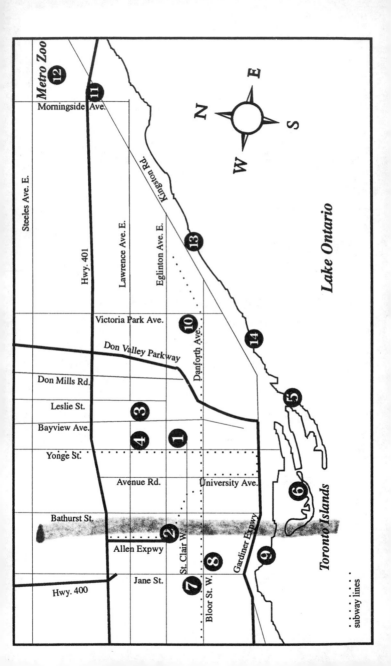

Contents

ISBN 0-920361-00-5

Copyright © 1984, 1985, 1987, 1990, 1993, 1994 and 1996
Revised edition 1996
All rights reserved

Printed in Canada
Tenth printing 1996

Published by:
Great North Books
60 Bayhampton Crescent
Thornhill, Ontario
Canada L4J 7G9

Trade distribution by:
Firefly Books Ltd.
3680 Victoria Park Avenue
Willowdale, Ontario
Canada M2H 3K1

Introduction

Within easy reach of everyone living in or visiting Toronto, but unknown to many, are scenic country trails for walking, exploring, picnics, birdwatching, bicycling and cross-country skiing. These paths refresh us with needed contact with nature, away from the stress of city living. Immersed in these natural worlds, many of them virtually minutes away, you walk a forest trail beside a gurgling brook, along grassy river banks, through gullies and along spectacular wild shores washed by the waves of Lake Ontario. You can see birds, animals, bursting wildflowers in spring and the colors of the leaves in autumn.

How to reach Toronto's best country walks by T.T.C. public transit or by automobile, the route, and how to get back to the subway or your car from the walk's end are fully detailed here. With this book, you can explore and experience one of these hidden natural treasures every weekend.

Using this book

Each country walk is accompanied by a map for you to follow using the detailed directions in the text. Not all the streets are included on the map, just those needed to help you find your way. Don't let this book sit on your shelf. Put on comfortable walking shoes, pack a snack and go!

1. Rosedale

5 km/3 miles
Located within minutes of the center of Toronto, the wooded Rosedale ravines offer walking, running and cross-country skiing.

Every day thousands of people work or shop on Yonge Street near these nature trails but most are unaware of the diverse wildlife, forests, spring wildflowers and flowing brooks that are so close — great for a relaxing lunchtime stroll.

PUBLIC TRANSIT: From the St. Clair subway station (on the Yonge Street line), walk north on Yonge Street. Turn right on Heath Street East and walk to the end of the street. Here is a sign reading "Nature Trail," and the start of the walk.

AUTOMOBILE: Drive to the corner of Yonge Street and Heath Street East, just north of St. Clair Avenue. Go east on Heath Street East to the end of the street to a sign reading "Nature Trail." Parking in this area can be difficult, and you would probably be better off taking public transit.

THE WALK: Follow the arrow of the "Nature Trail" sign and descend the steps into the ravine. At the bottom turn right and follow the path along the brook, called Yellow Creek. Pass under the St. Clair Avenue bridge, and after crossing a wooden footbridge enter David Balfour Park. Going south through Balfour Park you pass under the Summerhill railroad bridge and soon reach busy Mount Pleasant Road. Carefully cross Mount Pleasant Road — there is no traffic light — and follow the path indicated by the "Park Drive Reservation" sign.

You soon reach a trail junction. If you want to end the walk, you can take the path leading to Creighleigh Gardens and take Milkman's Road to South Drive. From there you can take the Rosedale 82 bus to Rosedale subway station (on the Yonge Street line), or the Sherbourne 75A bus to the Sherbourne station (on the Bloor-Danforth line).

To continue this walk, go left at this junction and follow the sign to Moore Park Ravine. The path enters the Don Valley and skirts a Bayview Avenue ramp. You also pass the old Don Valley Brick Works, founded in 1882. Near it is the pit from which the clay was taken to be made into bricks. The trail goes near the fence around the pit which measures 30 meters (100 feet) deep and 150 meters (500 feet) from end to end.

Follow the path north along a ridge through the maples and willows of Moore Park ravine and gradually ascend to Moore Avenue.

GETTING BACK: From Moore Avenue, cross the street and take the South Leaside 88 bus back to your starting point at the St. Clair subway station.

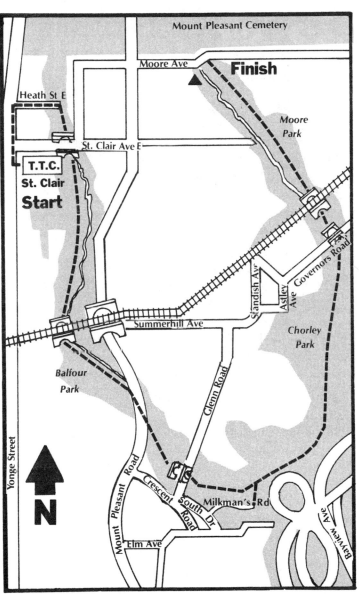

Mount Pleasant Cemetery

Moore Ave

Finish

Heath St E

Moore Park

St. Clair Ave E

T.T.C.
St. Clair
Start

Standish Ave

Ashley Ave

Governors Road

Summerhill Ave

Chorley Park

Balfour Park

Glenn Road

Yonge Street

N

Mount Pleasant Road

Crescent South Dr Road

Milkman's Rd

Bayview Ave

Elm Ave

⬆ = Washrooms   ▲ = Water Fountain

Saving the Rosedale Ravine

Toronto is fortunate to have wooded ravines that are freely accessible to everyone. But the preservation of these ravines in their natural state was not always guaranteed. In February 1955, a Rosedale resident learned that Kensington Industries had bought land on the edge of the ravine and planned to construct an apartment building with a rear descent of 38 meters (125 feet) into the ravine. Their split-level building would have three storeys on the table-land and nine storeys anchored to the ravine wall. The law then in force limited the height of buildings on the table-land to 10 meters (35 feet), but it did not mention descent into the ravine. The developers were going to build their apartments in the idyllic wooded ravines that had been preserved due to 25 years of work by conservationists.

A "Save the Ravines" group was formed. They publicized the threat to the ravines and campaigned for the municipal government to bring a halt to the construction plans. On February 21st, 1955, work crews began cutting trees in the ravine. On February 28th Mayor Nathan Phillips and the Board of Controllers met with the conservationists and the developers, and voted against allowing the construction. That same day the City Council voted to expropriate the Rosedale ravine to preserve its natural character for future generations.

2. Cedarvale Ravine

2.4 km / 1.5 miles

Walking, running, cycling and cross-country skiiing in a wooded ravine. Lights along the path allow for evening walks.

Over 30 species of birds nest in the Cedarvale ravine. During the spring and fall, many migrating birds can be seen here. Among the species that can be observed are Cardinals, Great Horned Owls, Barred Owls, Long-eared Owls and several species of finches. In winter, birds are attracted by the feeding stations in the nearby gardens.

Flowing through the Cedarvale ravine is Castle Frank Brook, named after the summer residence of Lieutenant Governor John Simcoe and his wife. In her diary Mrs. Simcoe wrote: "We found the river very shallow in many parts and obstructed by trees. A bald eagle sat on a blasted pine on a very bald point."

In the late 1960s and early 1970s the Cedarvale ravine was part of the proposed route of the Spadina Expressway, In June 1971 organized protests halted Spadina Expressway construction and the destruction of this ravine.

PUBLIC TRANSIT: Go to Eglinton West subway station (on the Spadina line), and exit onto Eglinton Avenue West. Walk to the right and cross Eglinton Avenue and then go to the left on Eglinton Avenue. Turn right on Everden Road and walk down this street to Ava Road. Here is the path leading through Cedarvale Park to the Cedarvale ravine.

AUTOMOBILE: Park your car on a street near Eglinton West subway station, which is located on Eglinton Avenue West, west of Bathurst Street, and then follow the above directions.

THE WALK: Follow the path through Cedarvale Park to the wide and deep Cedarvale ravine. The path through the ravine follows Castle Frank Brook and goes under the Glen Cedar Road bridge, and the Bathurst Street bridge. The path eventually ascends to Heath Street West and an entrance (by cash or tokens only) to the St. Clair West subway station (on the Spadina line), one stop south of this walk's starting point at Eglinton West subway station.

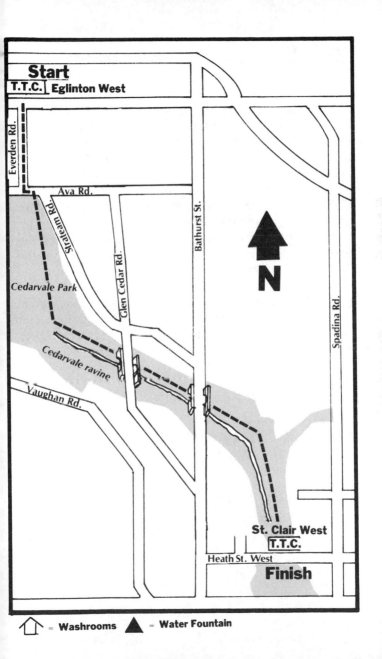

Mrs. Simcoe and her diary

As someone who loved to walk in the outdoors, Elizabeth Simcoe explored and gave names to many of the natural areas described in this book. In 1791, at age 25, Elizabeth Simcoe left Wolford, her 5,000 acre estate in Devonshire, England, and came here with her husband John Graves Simcoe who had been appointed Lieutenant-Governor of Upper Canada (which later became the province of Ontario).

Mrs. Simcoe faced life in the Canadian wilderness with enthusiasm. She travelled extensively in the Toronto (then called York), Niagara, Queenston and Gananoque areas and recorded her impressions in her diary. The daily entries and her sketches vividly depict the land and life in Ontario's early pioneering days. Her drawings are among the earliest pictorial records available of the area. In 1796 the Simcoes returned to England and their estate at Wolford.

John Graves Simcoe   *Elizabeth Simcoe*

J.R. Robertson Collection, Metropolitan Toronto Library

3.Wilket Creek-E.T. Seton Park

5 km/3 miles

Walking, cycling, running and cross-country skiing through the valleys of Wilket Creek and the West Don River, one of the largest natural areas in Toronto. This walk can be combined with the Taylor Creek walk for a total of 10 km (6 miles) ending at the Victoria Park subway station (on the Bloor-Danforth line).

A great variety of birds can be seen on this very scenic walk. It is especially beautiful in the spring when migrating birds are here among the bursting spring wildflowers. The starting point at Edwards Gardens, formerly part of the estate of wealthy paint manufacturer Rupert Edwards, is landscaped with floral displays and rock gardens. The slopes of the ravine are covered with colorful flowers, plants, shrubs and trees. The rock gardens contain 426 tons of Credit Valley stone. (Bicycles are not permitted in Edwards Gardens so cyclists should use the cinder path from Leslie Street down to Wilket Creek Park.)

Wilket Creek is a narrow wooded park where abundant birdlife can be seen. Its natural state contrasts with the manicured Edwards Gardens. The West Don River flows through the wide open valley of E.T. Seton Park, named after the world-famous artist-naturalist and author whose love of nature was inspired here in the 1870s.

PUBLIC TRANSIT: From the Eglinton subway station (on the Yonge Street line), take the Lawrence East 54 bus to Edwards Gardens at Leslie Street and Lawrence Avenue East.

AUTOMOBILE: Edwards Gardens is located on Lawrence Avenue East, just west of the intersection of Leslie Street. The entrance to the parking lot is on Leslie Street just south of Lawrence Avenue.

THE WALK: After enjoying the floral displays of Edwards Gardens, take a path down into the ravine. When you reach the creek go left towards the sign for Wilket Creek Park. Soon after entering Wilket Creek Park, you come to a sign indicating that it's 1.5 km (about 1 mile) to Eglinton Avenue East. Reaching the park road leading to Eglinton Avenue East, you can end the walk here by walking out to the street and taking one of the buses going west on Eglinton Avenue to Eglinton subway station (on the Yonge Street line).

To continue the walk, turn left on the park road and go under the Eglinton Avenue East bridge. Cross the concrete footbridge over the creek and continue south into E.T. Seton Park. Pass under the C.P. Railway trestle. You soon reach a side path leading up to Don Mills Road, from where you can take the Don Mills 25 bus to Pape subway station (on the Bloor-Danforth line).

Continuing south through E.T. Seton Park, you pass under the Overlea Boulevard bridge and eventually reach a sign reading "Edwards Gardens 5 km, Sunnybrook Park 5 km." If you want to continue on the Taylor Creek walk, go to the left here and follow that walk. Otherwise go right and follow the road parallel to the railway tracks. Then turn right up the hill leading to Thorncliffe Park Drive.

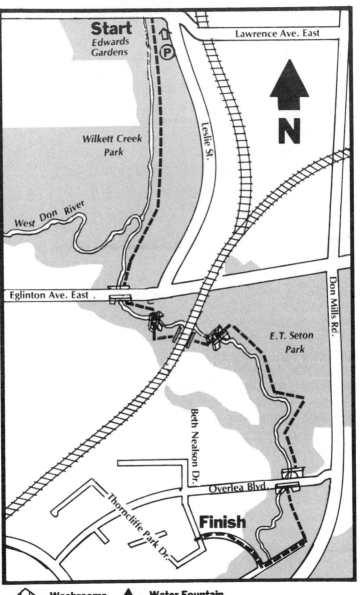

= Washrooms ⌂   **= Water Fountain** ▲

GETTING BACK: To your right on Thorncliffe Park Drive is the stop for the Thorncliffe Park 81 bus, which goes to Pape subway station (on the Bloor-Danforth line). The bus stops on this side of the street after 3:30 p.m. Before 3:30 p.m. it circles Thorncliffe Park Drive on the other side of the street.

Or, on weekdays and Saturdays you can take the South Leaside 88 bus from either side of Thorncliffe Park Drive (take the bus that comes first) to St. Clair subway station (on the Yonge Street line).

To get back to Edwards Gardens, walk out to, but don't cross Overlea Boulevard, and take the Don Mills 25 bus east along Overlea Boulevard and north on Don Mills Road to Lawrence Avenue East. Then take the Lawrence East 54 bus west to Leslie Street.

Metropolitan Toronto Library

E.T. Seton

Ernest Thompson Seton

Artist-naturalist and author Ernest Thompson Seton explored the wilderness of the Don River Valley in the 1870s. His books based in part on his experiences and observations here became famous world-wide best-sellers. Born in 1860 in South Shields, Durham, England, E.T. Seton immigrated with his family to Canada in 1866, settling in Toronto in 1870.

Ernest built a small cabin in the woods near the Don River where he retreated after school and on weekends to collect shells and feathers and live a Robinson Crusoe-type life. "To a small boy, as I was then, it was a wild and distant country. To me, it was paradise," he later wrote.

He enrolled in the Ontario College of Art and at age 19 won the college's Gold Medal. He then went to study in England, where he spent many days at the natural history collection of the British Museum, visiting the London Zoo and starving due to lack of money.

Back in Canada, Seton began writing simple but moving stories about the adventures and personalities of animals he watched in the Don Valley. Silverspot was a wise old crow who taught the other crows in the valley the tricks of keeping safe from armed men and horned owls. Seton observed a mother partridge, pretending to be injured, flapping along the ground just out of reach of Reynard the fox, distracting him from her little chick Redruff.

In 1898 these two stories plus six others were published in *Wild Animals I Have Known*, the first of Seton's 40 books. It was sold out within three weeks, and during the next eight years was reprinted 20 times. It has since appeared in at least 15 English language editions and 15 foreign editions.

Rudyard Kipling's Jungle Books were inspired by Seton's stories, and American President and naturalist Theodore Roosevelt was one of Seton's greatest admirers.

Seton later moved to the United States and was chief of the Boy Scouts of America from 1910 to 1915. He died on October 23, 1946 at the age of 86 at his 2,500 acre ranch in New Mexico.

4. Sherwood Park

5.5 km/3.4 miles
Walking, running and cross-country skiing through a rustic valley in one of the largest natural areas in Toronto.

Starting at the beautiful floral displays of the Alexander Muir Gardens, this walk takes you through the thick forests of a tributary of the West Don River. One section is wild and you have to find your way along a narrow path. At pastoral Sunnybrook Park the route turns north through the forests along the West Don River and emerges at the Glendon College campus of York University. The West Don River is a major tributary of the Don River, named by Lieutenant-Governor John Graves Simcoe after the Don River in central England.

PUBLIC TRANSIT: From Lawrence subway station (on the Yonge Street line), exit to the northeast corner of the intersection of Lawrence Avenue and Yonge Street. Cross Lawrence Avenue and continue south on Yonge Street to St. Edmunds Drive and the Alexander Muir Memorial Gardens.

AUTOMOBILE: Park your car on a side street near Yonge Street and Lawrence Avenue. Walk south on Yonge Street to St. Edmunds Drive and the Alexander Muir Memorial Gardens.

THE WALK: Enter Alexander Muir Gardens, go down the steps and walk through the gardens. Follow the path to the road. Go left, walk to the end of the road and take the path into the ravine.

The path goes under the Mount Pleasant Road bridge and eventually ascends at Blythwood Road. Cross Blythwood Road to the "Nature Trail" sign and descend into the ravine. After passing a children's playground, another "Nature Trail" sign indicates the trail turns left. Climb the wooden steps up the hillside. The path eventually emerges at Bayview Avenue.

Go left on Bayview Avenue. Cross Bayview Avenue at the traffic lights at Blythwood Road and enter the grounds of Sunnybrook Hospital. At the first stop sign, go right. Then turn left and walk on the sidewalk. Follow the road as it curves around to the left. Go right on the road marked "Dead End, No Exit" through a wooded area to a bridge over the West Don River.

From here, if you want to reach the Wilket Creek-E.T. Seton Park walk: cross the bridge, turn right at sign indicating "Eglinton Avenue and TTC" and follow the park road.

To continue this walk, don't cross the bridge, but go to your left and take the path marked by a brown post with a pink top. Follow the path along the river. You eventually reach the playing fields at Glendon College. Walk to the end of the field and go left along the dirt road to a paved road.

GETTING BACK: Go straight on the road. At the "One Way Do Not Enter" sign, go left up the staircase and then right, through the college to Bayview Avenue. Cross Lawrence Avenue and take the Bayview 11 or Davisville 28B bus to Lawrence subway station (on the Yonge Street Line), this walk's start.

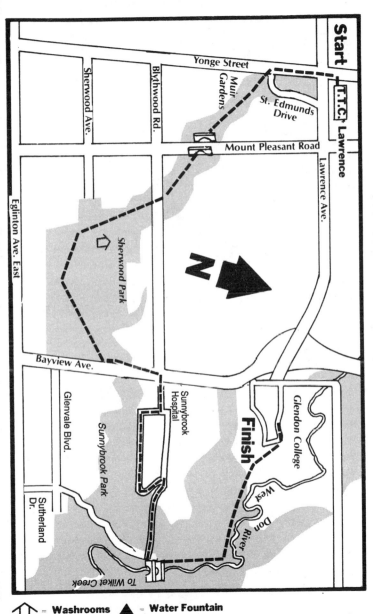

Start

T.T.C. Lawrence

Yonge Street

Sherwood Ave.

Blythwood Rd.

Muir Gardens

St. Edmunds Drive

Mount Pleasant Road

Lawrence Ave.

N

Eglinton Ave. East

Sherwood Park

Bayview Ave.

Glenvale Blvd.

Sunnybrook Park

Sunnybrook Hospital

Finish

Glendon College

Don River West

Sutherland Dr.

To Wilket Creek

⇧ = Washrooms   ▲ = Water Fountain

5. Tommy Thompson Park

10 km/6 miles return

Lagoons, beaches and wildflowers are found in 189-hectare (466 acres) Tommy Thompson Park — also known as the Leslie Street Spit — which juts into Lake Ontario from south of Leslie Street and extends beyond the eastern end of the Toronto Islands. The 5-km (3 miles) long headland offers walking, cycling and running. A cool breeze blows off the lake during the summer.

The more than 40 hectares (100 acres) of lagoons on the headland are the home or stopover for migrating sandpipers and the largest colony of ring-billed seagulls in the world. It has also attracted a breeding colony of terns, as well as other species of geese, seagulls and ducks.

In 1985 the headland was named Tommy Thompson Park after Metro Toronto's popular first Parks Commissioner. Thompson was well known for his "Please Walk on the Grass" signs and the walks he led in Toronto's natural areas.

HOURS: Tommy Thompson Park is open weekends and holidays from 9 a.m. to 6 p.m. during spring, summer and fall. A special bus service along the headland runs hourly from 10 a.m. to 5 p.m. The return trip leaves from the end of the headland on the half hour from 10:30 to 5:30. During spring and summer the bus service starts at Queen Street East and Leslie Street. After Labour Day, a mini-bus departs from the main gate at Unwin Avenue and Leslie Street. For any changes, call the Metro Toronto and Region Conservation Authority at (416) 661-6600.

PUBLIC TRANSIT: Take the Queen Street streetcar from Queen subway station (on the Yonge Street line) or Osgoode subway station (on the University line) to Leslie Street, and take the special bus that goes along the headland or walk south on Leslie Street.

AUTOMOBILE: Drive along Lake Shore Boulevard East, which is located under the Gardiner Expressway, and turn south down Leslie Street toward the lake. There is parking along Leslie Street and Unwin Avenue.

THE WALK: After passing through the gate at the corner of Leslie Street and Unwin Avenue, walk south on Leslie Street which soon connects with the roadway along the headland. After about 1.5 km (1 mile) there is a path on your right which leads to the sandy beach which is supervised for swimming.

The main route continues to the end of the headland where the path climbs to the Toronto Harbour Lighthouse. From this vantage point you have a tremendous view of the lagoons and on a clear day you can see the shores of the United States approximately 50 km (30 miles) away.

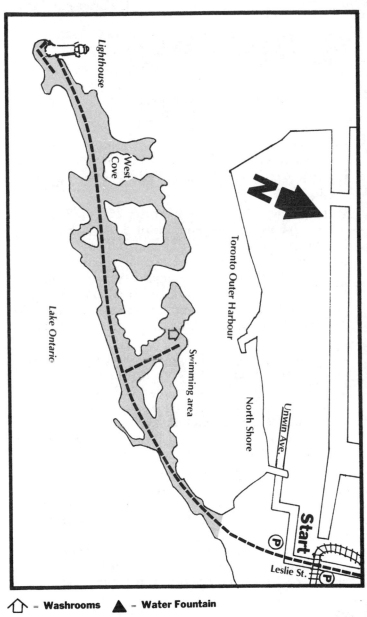

⌂ = Washrooms ▲ = Water Fountain

6. Toronto Islands

Ward's Island to Hanlan's Point 5.25 km/3.25 miles
Ward's Island to Centre Island 3.25 km/2 miles
Centre Island to Hanlan's Point 2 km/1.2 miles
Eight minutes away by ferry boat from downtown are the enchanting Toronto Islands, a chain of islands separated by channels and small bays. Within its 365 hectares (750 acres) of parkland are sandy beaches, sand dunes and forests offering walking, cycling and running. There is also fishing, canoeing and sailing here.

"The water in the bay is beautifully clear and transparent... The air on these sands is peculiarly clear and fine. The Indians esteem this place so healthy that they come and stay here when they are ill," wrote Mrs. Simcoe about this area. Lieutenant-Governor Simcoe chose Toronto as the provincial capital because he believed he could fortify the site and defend it from the American invasion. An important factor in the defense of Toronto were the military advantages offered by the Toronto Islands in guarding the city. Historical markers indicate the location of the military positions on the island.

The Toronto Islands were once a peninsula attached to Toronto but during a terrible storm in 1858 the waters of Lake Ontario broke through part of the peninsula and the islands were created. Among the abundant birdlife that can be seen are Canada geese, mallards, grackles, wrens, owls, ruby-throated hummingbirds, Black-crowned Night herons and snow geese. In late summer and fall, migrating shorebirds and one of the largest concentrations of Saw-whet owls in the world can been seen here. Fish found in the island's lagoons include alewives, yellow perch, bluegill, carp, northern pike, largemouth bass, rainbow trout and coho salmon. A pond stocked with trout is also available to anglers.

PUBLIC TRANSIT: Take either of the north-south subway lines to Union station. Transfer to the Harbourfront LRT and get off at Queens Quay station. The ferry terminal is on Queens Quay West at the foot of Bay Street just behind the Harbour Castle Westin Hotel.

AUTOMOBILE: There are parking lots along Queen's Quay near the ferry docks which are at the foot of Bay Street. During the summer finding a parking space may be difficult, and it would probably be best to leave your car at home or near a subway station and take the subway.

FERRIES: Ferry service is operated to Ward's Island, Centre Island and Hanlan's Point. For a tape recorded message giving current schedules and cost, call (416) 392-8193. Service is seasonal. During the summer there is service to all three points. The ferry to Ward's Island is the only one that operates year-round.

THE WALK: All the pathways on the Toronto Islands offer pleasant and relaxing country walking. Signs here read: "Please walk on the grass." The most scenic and wild walk is along the shore of Lake Ontario from Ward's Island to Hanlan's Point. You can take the ferry to any of the three points and walk to the lakeshore. As ferry service to Ward's Island operates year-round, this walk begins here.

From the Ward's Island ferry dock, follow the sign "To Boardwalk and Beach," and walk to the boardwalk. Go to the right and walk along the boardwalk and enjoy the view of the Outer Harbour Headland and Lake Ontario. In winter huge waves crash over the breakwater.

At Centre Island is a concrete pier extending into the lake. From here you can fish and watch the seagulls. Opposite the pier is the path across Centre Island to the Centre Island ferry dock.

Continue along the lakeshore to the Gibraltar Lighthouse, built in 1808. It is believed to be haunted by its first keeper who disappeared mysteriously in 1815. Part of a human skeleton was later found nearby.

Past the lighthouse is a well-stocked pond where you can fish for trout. Beyond the pond, take the path onto the sand dunes on the lakeshore. These driftwood-strewn beaches are the wildest section of the walk. Hike all the way to the fence at the end of the beach and walk to the right to Hanlan's Point, named for the family of world-champion sculler Ned Hanlan who lived here and was elected alderman in 1898 and 1899. The area was originally known as Gibraltar Point as it guarded the entrance to the harbour of Toronto. By 1800 there were two storehouses and a guard house here which were destroyed by the Americans during their second raid on the city in 1813 during the War of 1812-14.

Walk to the Hanlan's Point ferry dock. From here take the ferry back to the mainland, or you can walk back to the Centre Island ferry or to the Ward's Island ferry.

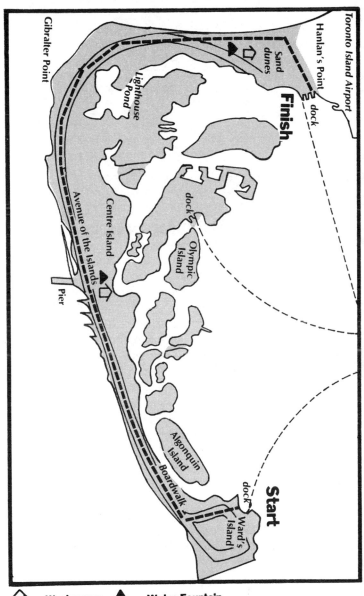

Toronto Island Airport

Hanlan's Point

Gibralter Point

Sand dunes

Finish

dock

Lighthouse Pond

Avenue of the Islands

Centre Island

dock

Olympic Island

Pier

Algonquin Island

Boardwalk

dock

Start

Ward's Island

⬆ = **Washrooms**   ▲ = **Water Fountain**

7. Humber River Valley

6.25 km/3.9 miles

One of Toronto's major river valleys, the wooded and steep-walled Humber River Valley offers picturesque walking, cycling, running and cross-country skiing. Ducks swim in the river and shorebirds, seagulls and migrant birds can be seen here in the spring and autumn.

In the twilight after sundown on September 9th, 1615, a 23-year-old explorer named Etienne Brule looked out over Lake Ontario at the mouth of the Humber River, and became the first European to see Lake Ontario. Accompanied by twelve Huron Indians, Brule had travelled from their village on Lake Simcoe down the 45-km (28 miles) portage route known as the Toronto Carrying-Place Trail along the Humber River Valley to Lake Ontario.

The Toronto Carrying-Place Trail from Lake Simcoe and Georgian Bay to Lake Ontario was well-travelled by the Indians who gave the name Toronto, which meant "carrying place" or "meeting place," to the area at the mouth of the Humber River. This trail was used by explorers, missionaries and traders until Lieutenant Governor John Simcoe built Yonge Street in 1796. Simcoe named the river after the Humber River in Devonshire, on the North Sea.

Public Archives of Canada C-73635

Etienne Brule at the mouth of the Humber River on Lake Ontario from a drawing by C.W. Jeffreys.

PUBLIC TRANSIT: Take the subway to the Old Mill station (on the Bloor-Danforth line). Exit from the station onto Humber Boulevard and go right. Turn right again on Old Mill Road. As you walk down the hill, the remains of the Old Mill are on your right. Made of stones quarried from the Humber River Valley, this mill dates from 1848. Earlier sawmills were located here for cutting lumber to build the new settlement of York which later became the city of Toronto. Cross the Old Mill Bridge, built in 1916, and descend the stairs on your left to the path along the Humber River.

AUTOMOBILE: From Bloor Street West, turn north onto Humber Boulevard, located several streets west of

Jane Street. Go right on Old Mill Road. Cross the Old Mill Bridge and turn left at the entrance to Etienne Brule Park. The path is at the parking lot.

THE WALK: The path follows the banks of the Humber River through Etienne Brule Park. Here are picnic tables, barbecue pits and washroom facilities. Just before the Dundas Street bridge a path on the right leads up to Dundas Street from where you can take the Lambton 30 bus east to the High Park subway station or west to the Kipling subway station (both on the Bloor-Danforth line).

North of the Dundas Street bridge, the path goes through wooded Lambton Park and comes to a long footbridge across the Humber River. On the bridge are benches for you to sit and enjoy the view of the river.

Past the bridge the path goes under a railway trestle and then through a very wooded area, emerging at James Gardens. Here are picnic tables and barbecue pits. On the other side of the Humber River is a golf course and the point where Black Creek flows into the Humber River. A trail sign a bit farther north indicates washrooms are ¼ km to the left.

Follow the path under the Scarlett Road bridge. (In winter the path under the bridge is closed and it is necessary to cross the road.) The path then goes through open parkland to the corner of Eglinton Avenue West and Scarlett Road.

GETTING BACK: Reaching Eglinton Avenue West, cross Scarlett Road and take the Eglinton 32 or 32B bus east to the Eglinton West subway station (on the Spadina line). If you are going back to your car near Old Mill, take the Scarlett 79 bus to the Runnymede subway station (on the Bloor-Danforth line) and go west for two stops to Old Mill station.

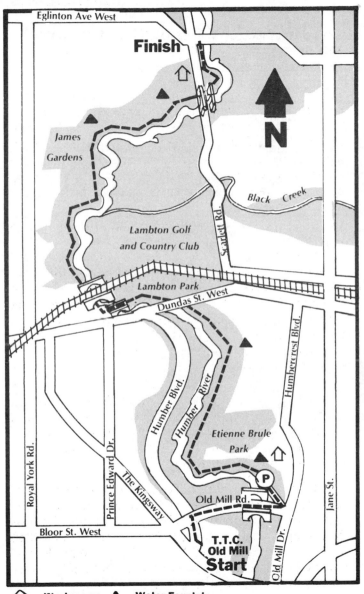

Eglinton Ave West

Finish

N

James
Gardens

Black Creek

Lambton Golf
and Country Club

Scarlett Rd.

Lambton Park

Dundas St. West

Humber Blvd.

Humber River

Humbercrest Blvd.

Etienne Brule
Park

Royal York Rd.

Prince Edward Dr.

The Kingsway

Old Mill Rd.

P

Bloor St. West

**T.T.C.
Old Mill
Start**

Old Mill Dr.

Jane St.

⬆ = **Washrooms**   ▲ - **Water Fountain**

The saga of Etienne Brule

The youthful discoverer of the Humber River Valley, Etienne Brule, was born near Paris, France in 1592 and came to Quebec with Samuel de Champlain in 1608. He was exchanged for a Huron whom Champlain took back to France. After spending the winter of 1610-11 with the Indians, Brule adopted Indian ways and remained with the Hurons until 1615. He then acted as Champlain's interpreter. Champlain promised to help the Hurons attack the Iroquois if the Hurons accepted a missionary. The Hurons wanted assistance from the Andastes, on the Susquehanna River, for the battle with the Iroquois. It was on this mission that Brule and his twelve companions made their historic voyage on the Humber River Valley route. But by the time the Andastes returned with Brule, the Hurons had been defeated.

Etienne Brule's accomplishments were many. He was the first European to speak the languages of the Algonquin and Huron Indians, and the first to journey from Quebec to Lake Huron by way of the Ottawa River. Brule was the first white man to enter what is now the province of Ontario and the first to explore the shores of Lake Superior. He was also the first to traverse northern New York and descend the Susquehanna River through Pennsylvania and Maryland.

In spite of his many discoveries, Brule was not well regarded in his time. The Jesuit missionaries considered his living with the Hurons and adopting their ways as a disgrace to the French and to Christianity. Brule's life ended in 1633 when he was murdered and eaten by his former Huron friends. His remains are believed to be buried according to Huron custom near the site of Penetanguishene, Ontario.

8. High Park

5 km/3 miles

Walking, cycling and running in a circuit route through the hills, forests and along streams and a lake in 137-hectare (339 acres) High Park.

Many species of waterfowl can be seen on High Park's Grenadier Pond, especially during the spring and autumn when many species of migrating ducks, seagulls, geese, grebes and swallows visit the park. You can also rent rowboats at the pond and fish in its well-stocked waters.

High Park was a gift to Toronto by John Howard, an architect who came to Toronto in 1832 and was made city surveyor by Toronto's first mayor William Lyon Mackenzie. In 1836 Howard bought 67 hectares (165 acres) here and built his home which he called Colborne Lodge after Sir John Colborne, then Lieutenant Governor of Ontario. Howard donated the property as a public park in 1873 and over the years additional land was added. Colborne Lodge is now a museum containing original furnishings including the kitchen and fireplace, and examples of early Canadian art.

PUBLIC TRANSIT: Go to the High Park subway station (on the Bloor-Danforth line) and exit onto High Park Avenue. Go to the right, down High Park Avenue and cross Bloor Street West to the entrance of High Park.

AUTOMOBILE: Drive along Bloor Street West and turn south into High Park through the entrance opposite High Park Avenue. Take the West Road and park in one of the designated lots. The park is closed to cars on weekends and holidays from May to September, so it's necessary to park along Bloor Street or High Park Avenue.

THE WALK: From the entrance to High Park, walk west along Bloor Street on the edge of the park to a sign reading "Nature Trail." Follow the arrow and walk on the path along the side of the ravine. Here the trees have signs indicating their species.

The trail gradually descends to the shore of Grenadier Pond, named for the British soldiers who used to do their drills on the frozen lake during winters in the mid-nineteenth century.

At the southern end of the pond, turn left and go along the path which emerges at The Queensway. If you want to end the walk here, cross The Queensway and get on the the Queen Street 501 streetcar which will take you to Osgoode subway station (on the University line), and then to Queen subway station (on the Yonge Street line).

To continue the walk, stay on the path, cross Colborne Lodge Drive and follow the path as it turns left back into High Park. The walk crosses Deer Pen Road where there is a refreshment stand and water fountain nearby. Follow the trail uphill as it parallels Spring Road and then as it gradually ascends out of the forest. Turn right on Colborne Lodge Drive to the park entrance. Cross Bloor Street West and walk up High Park Avenue to the High Park subway station.

OTHER ATTRACTIONS: Other facilities in High Park that you might want to visit include: 1. Colborne

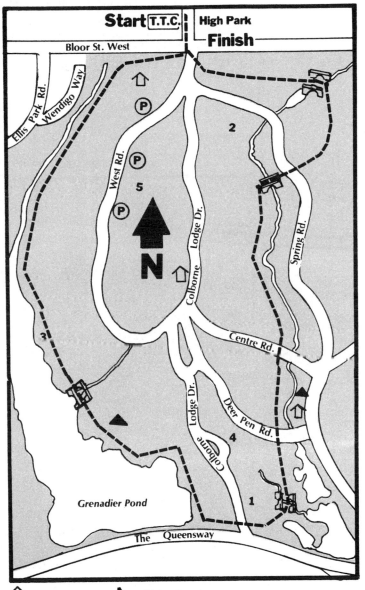

Start T.T.C. **High Park** **Finish**

Bloor St. West

Ellis Park Rd.

Wendigo Way

West Rd.

P

P

P

5

N

Colborne Lodge Dr.

2

Spring Rd.

Centre Rd.

3

Lodge Dr.

Colborne

4

Deer Pen Rd.

1

Grenadier Pond

The Queensway

⬆ = Washrooms ▲ = Water Fountain

Lodge: Open Monday to Saturday 9:30 a.m. to 5 p.m. and Sunday 1 p.m. to 5 p.m. 2. Sculpture Symposium Area. 3. The Bandstand, featuring free evening and Sunday afternoon concerts during the summer. 4. High Park Zoo. 5. Swimming Pool.

9. Sunnyside Beaches

4 km/2.5 miles one way

Walking, cycling and running through grassy parkland along the shores of Lake Ontario from the mouth of the Humber River west to Ontario Place. The western half of this route is along sandy and grass beaches while the eastern half is a walkway right on the lakeshore.

A cool breeze off Lake Ontario makes this a pleasant walk on a hot summer's day. Along the beach are picnic tables, a swimming pool and a playground for children. Just offshore is a breakwater which is a favourite resting place for ducks and gulls including some uncommon species such as Glaucous Gulls, Iceland Gulls, Herring Gulls and Great Black-backed Gulls. During the spring and fall, migrating terns can also be seen here.

PUBLIC TRANSIT: Take the subway to Dundas West station (on the Bloor-Danforth line) and take the 504 streetcar down Roncesvalles Avenue to The Queensway. Get off the streetcar here, cross The Queensway to the walkway over the Gardiner Expressway. This brings you to the Palais Royale Ballroom at approximately the mid-point of the Sunnyside Beaches walk.

AUTOMOBILE: The Sunnyside Beaches are along Lake Shore Boulevard West. Parking lots are located at the foot of Windermere Avenue, and at the foot of Ellis

Avenue, at the western end of the walk near the mouth of the Humber River.

THE WALK: This walk is divided into two sections. The western section, to your right if you came via the walkway from the foot of Roncesvalles Avenue, is grassy parkland with sandy beaches. Walk right along the water and enjoy the beautiful blue colour of Lake Ontario. Along your way is a monument with railroad tracks honouring Sir Casimir Gzowski, a Polish exile and creative engineer who was co-founder of the company that built the Grand Trunk Railway between Toronto and Sarnia, and constructed the International Bridge across the Niagara River in the 1870s. He was also the first chairman of the Niagara Falls Parks Commission and planned the park system along the Canadian side which today provides much enjoyment for the many thousands of visitors to Niagara Falls.

At the western end of this walk near the mouth of the Humber River is the Lion Monument. It was erected here in August 1940 at the entrance to the Queen Elizabeth Way to commemorate its opening in 1939 by Queen Elizabeth and King George VI on the first trip of the British Sovereign to Canada.

Going east from the walkway at the foot of Roncesvalles Avenue, the path parallels Lake Shore Boulevard West and goes past the Boulevard Club, the Toronto Sailing and Canoe Club and the Argonaut Rowing Club. Just past here are stairs down to Aquatic Drive, a walkway right along Lake Ontario's scenic shore. Walk this path to just outside of Ontario Place and turn back.

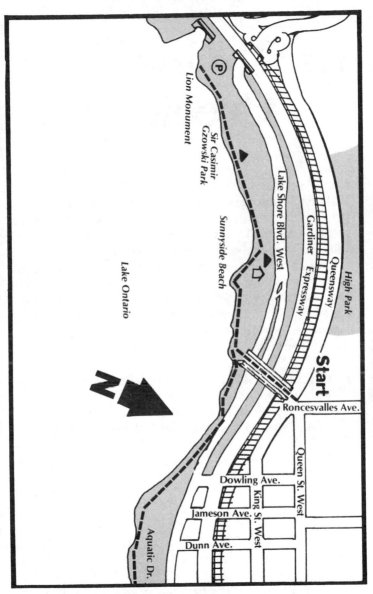

Lion Monument

Sir Casimir Gzowski Park

Sunnyside Beach

Lake Ontario

Lake Shore Blvd. West

Gardiner Expressway

Queensway

High Park

Start

Roncesvalles Ave.

Queen St. West

Dowling Ave.

King St. West

Jameson Ave.

Dunn Ave.

Aquatic Dr.

N

⬆ = **Washrooms**   ▲ = **Water Fountain**

10. Taylor Creek

5 km/3 miles

Walking, running, cycling and cross-country skiing through the wooded Taylor Creek valley to the forks of the Don river. This walk can be combined with the Wilket Creek walk for a total of 10 km (6 miles).

Though within the 344 square km (133 square miles) area drained by the Don River is now the highest average density of population in Canada, the wooded valley of Taylor Creek, a major tributary of the Don, is a peaceful respite where over 200 species of birds have been observed.

PUBLIC TRANSIT: Ride the Bloor-Danforth subway to Victoria Park station and exit onto Victoria Park Avenue. Turn right and walk down Victoria Park Avenue. Cross to the west side of the street at the traffic lights at Crescent Town Road and continue to a wooden sign reading "Sunnybrook Park 10 km, Edwards Gardens 10 km." Turn left here and go down the wooden stairs.

AUTOMOBILE: There are parking lots at both ends of the walk. To reach the end near Victoria Park Road, drive along Danforth Avenue and turn north on Dawes Road (several streets west of Victoria Park Road), and take the turn-off for the park just before the bridge over

the creek. Begin walking from the parking lot, which is just a short distance west of the Victoria Park Road.

To reach the other end of this walk, take the Don Valley Parkway and exit for Don Mills Road North. Keep to the right on the curve of the cloverleaf and take the first exit on the right marked "Taylor Creek Park." Follow the road under the Parkway to a parking lot next to the path.

THE WALK: After descending the steps from Victoria Park Road, follow the path. Go under the Dawes Road bridge and cross a wooden footbridge over a small stream to picnic tables, barbecue pits and washroom facilities. Wooden bridges at several places along the trail permit you to walk the path on either side of the creek. Fitness trail signs are posted along the path.

Before the O'Connor Drive bridge is a path leading up to O'Connor Drive. If you want to end the hike here you can take the Woodbine 91 bus to Woodbine subway station, or the O'Connor 70 bus to Coxwell subway station (both on the Bloor-Danforth line).

Continuing along the path, you come to a water fountain and public washrooms just before the O'Connor Drive bridge. When you reach a parking lot, you are near the end of Taylor Creek. This area is known as the forks of the Don as several of the river's tributaries converge here. Follow the signs left for Sunnybrook Park and Edwards Gardens, and walk across the arched concrete narrow bridge. Climb the hill and cross the wooden bridge over the railway tracks. After crossing, don't go up the wooden stairs in front of you, but turn left and go along the wooden walkway under Don Mills Road. Walk straight to a sign reading "Edwards Gardens 5 km, Sunnybrook Park 5 km." If you want to continue on the Wilket Creek walk, go right here and follow that walk. Otherwise turn left here and follow the road parallel to the railway tracks. Then turn right up the hill leading to Thorncliffe Park Drive. A sign here reads: "E.T. Seton Park, Central Don."

GETTING BACK: To your right on Thorncliffe Park Drive is the Thorncliffe Park 81 bus, which goes to the Pape subway station (on the Bloor-Danforth line). It stops on this side of the street after 3:30 p.m. Before

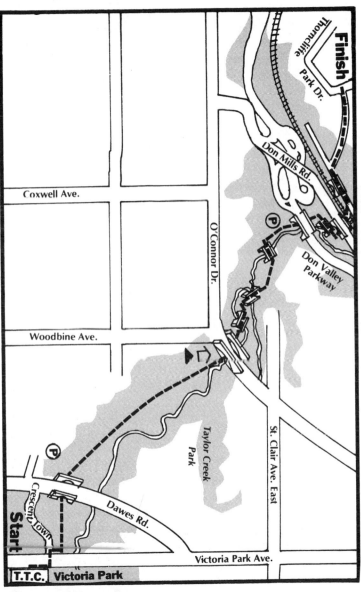

Coxwell Ave.

Woodbine Ave.

O'Connor Dr.

Don Mills Rd.

Don Valley Parkway

Thorncliffe Park Dr.

Finish

Taylor Creek Park

St. Clair Ave. East

Dawes Rd.

Crescent Town

Start

Victoria Park Ave.

 T.T.C.   **Victoria Park**

⌂ = Washrooms   ▲ = Water Fountain

3:30 p.m. it circles Thorncliffe Park Drive on the other side of the street. If you left your car near the Victoria Park Road end of the walk, take the subway from Pape station east to Victoria Park station.

Or, on weekdays and Saturdays you can take the South Leaside 88 bus from either side of Thorncliffe Park Drive (take the bus that comes first) to St. Clair subway station (on the Yonge Street line).

11. Highland Creek

5.5 km/3.5 miles

A wide creek flowing through a wooded rural area offering walking, bicycling, running and cross-country skiing.

In the 1830s when this area was settled for farming, 86-tonne (95 tons) schooners navigated almost a kilometer and a half (about one mile) up Highland Creek. Large stands of pine and hardwood trees supplied the saw mills. Trout could be caught in the streams. Although most of the farms are gone and the creek is not as wide and deep as 150 years ago, the walk along Highland Creek retains its rural character.

PUBLIC TRANSIT: Take the subway to the Kennedy station (on the Bloor-Danforth line). From there take the Scarboro 86 bus to the junction of Kingston Road and Old Kingston Road and walk down Old Kingston Road. Just past the "Welcome to Colonel Danforth Park, Highland Creek" sign is a parking lot. The walk begins here.

AUTOMOBILE: Take Lawrence Avenue East and go northeast on Kingston Road. Go left onto Old Kingston Road and down the hill to the parking lot just after the "Welcome to Colonel Danforth Park, Highland Creek" sign. Park your car here.

THE WALK: From the parking lot, pass through the gap in the log fence and follow the path. Turn left when you reach the main trail along Highland Creek. You soon pass a cow barn on your left. Cross the concrete footbridge over the creek. You then come to another footbridge but stay on the main path on your side of the creek.

After passing under the Morningside Avenue bridge and crossing a wooden footbridge, you enter Morningside Park which has picnic tables and washroom facilities. It's a good place to stop and eat the snacks from your pack.

The trail meanders along the creek and eventually emerges near an old house. Keep on the trail as it skirts the road here and goes back into the woods and descends to the creek. Just before the Lawrence Avenue bridge ascend the hill on the left to the street.

GETTING BACK: From Lawrence Avenue East stay on the same side of the street and take the Lawrence East 54 bus west to Lawrence East station (on the Scarborough Rapid Transit line). Take the Scarborough Rapid Transit to Kennedy station (on the Bloor-Danforth line).

If you have to get back to your car at the beginning of the walk, cross the street and take the Lawrence East 54 bus east to Kingston Road and then take the Scarboro 86 bus east to Old Kingston Road and walk down the hill to the parking lot.

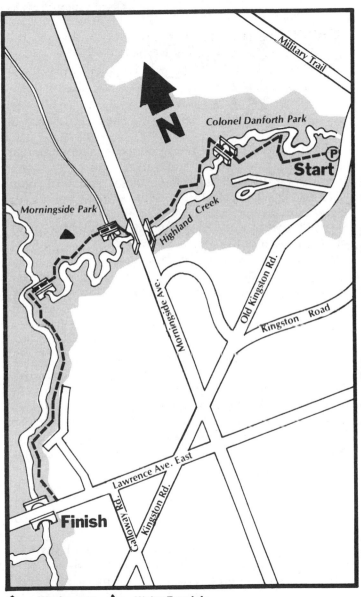

Military Trail

Colonel Danforth Park

P
Start

Morningside Park

Highland Creek

Morningside Ave.

Old Kingston Rd.

Kingston Road

Lawrence Ave. East

Galloway Rd.

Kingston Rd.

Finish

⌂ = **Washrooms**   ▲ = **Water Fountain**

12. Rouge River

6 km/3.75 miles

Flowing through one of the most wild areas within Toronto, the Rouge River takes a meandering course through a wide wooded valley with abundant wildlife. Situated south of the Metro Toronto Zoo, this route offers very rustic country walking. There is also fishing in the river. Near the southern end of this route is a campground and horseback riding stables. From the walk's end it it possible, besides taking the T.T.C. bus, to take GO Transit direct to downtown. Call for the schedule before heading out (see the "Getting Back" section for more details).

In the days before the arrival of the Europeans, the Iroquois Indians who lived along the Rouge River called it Ganatsekwyagon, meaning "among the birches." After the Europeans came, the Rouge River, like the Humber River on the western side of Toronto, was a portage route for fur traders travelling from Lake Ontario to Georgian Bay. Until 1678 the Rouge River Portage Trail was used as much as the Humber River Trail. After the Humber became the established route for the Europeans, the Rouge River route continued to be used by the Indians.

The Rouge River Valley has a variety of diverse habitats that support wildlife. Birds here include Common pheasant, Ruffed grouse and American wood-

cock. Among the animal life is raccoon, red fox, cottontail rabbit, European hare, woodchuck, grey squirrel, red squirrel, muskrat, skunk, mink and weasel. Fish found in the river include rainbow and brook trout.

PUBLIC TRANSIT: This route starts a few minutes' walk south of the Metro Toronto Zoo. To get to the zoo, go to Kennedy subway station (on the Bloor-Danforth line) and take the Scarboro 86A bus. Or, from Sheppard subway station (on the Yonge Street line): on weekends and holidays take the Sheppard 85B bus all the way to the zoo; on weekdays take the Sheppard 85 bus to Sheppard Avenue East and Meadowvale Road, and then take the Scarboro 86A bus north to the zoo.

AUTOMOBILE: Take Highway 401 east, exit onto Meadowvale Road and follow the signs north to the zoo. You can leave your car in the zoo's parking lot or at the trailhead where there is space for about four cars.

THE WALK: From the bus stop at the zoo, walk south on Park Road along the zoo bicycle path to Kirkhams Road. Go right on Kirkhams Road and walk down to the bridge over the Rouge River. Cross the bridge and walk to the end of the guardrail on your left to several short posts in the ground and parking space for about four cars. Here is the beginning of the trail.

Follow the gravel path the short distance to the river, then go right under the Meadowvale Road bridge, and walk along the sandy and grassy shores of the Rouge River. After passing the open area crossed by power lines, the path goes into the forest. Keep on the path as it gradually climbs the hill and when you come to a trail on your left, follow it back down to the river shore. Going straight will take you out to the road.

The path reaches the Twin Rivers Drive bridge over the Rouge River. Cross the river here and continue south on the other side of the river. The path traverses sandy riverbank, forests and meadows. It may occasionally be difficult to find the path. When this happens, just follow the river. The path connects with horseback riding trails marked by wooden posts with orange-painted tops.

Just before the Kingston Road-Highway 2 bridge there is a footbridge over the Rouge River. Go over the footbridge and follow the path up to the parking lot. Continue up the road past Glen Rouge Camping and several public telephones, to Kingston Road which is also Highway 2. A sign here reads: "Glen Rouge Park, Rouge River."

GETTING BACK: Turn right on Kingston Road-Highway 2 and go past the Rouge Hill Stables, the source of the horses you may have met on the trail. Walk to the

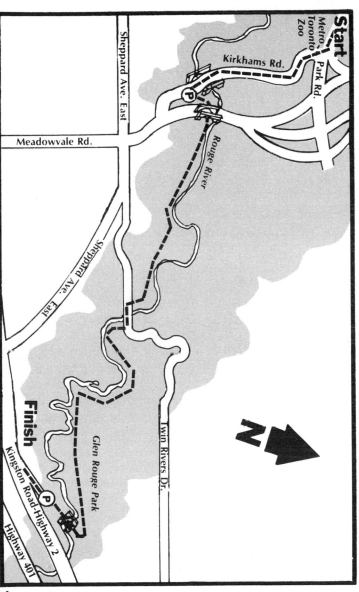

Start

Metro Toronto Zoo

Park Rd.

Kirkhams Rd.

Sheppard Ave. East

Meadowvale Rd.

Rouge River

Sheppard Ave. East

Twin Rivers Dr.

N

Finish

Kingston Road-Highway 2

Highway 401

Glen Rouge Park

⌂ = **Washrooms**   ▲ = **Water Fountain**

intersection of Sheppard Avenue East. From here, there are several ways to get back to downtown Toronto.

You can go right on Sheppard Avenue and take the Sheppard East 85A or 85E bus, which run on weekdays only, to Sheppard subway station (on the Yonge Street line). If you left your car at the zoo, you can get off at Sheppard Avenue East and Meadowvale Road and take the Scarboro 86A bus north to the zoo. On weekends and holidays only, you can take the Sheppard East 85D bus back to the zoo. From Meadowvale and Sheppard you can also take the Scarboro 86 bus south to Kennedy subway station (on the Bloor-Danforth line).

On Kingston Road-Highway 2 at Sheppard Avenue East is a bus stop for the GO Transit bus to GO bus stations at York Mills subway station (on the Yonge Street line) and Yorkdale subway station (on the Spadina line). It's also possible to take the GO train from the Rouge Hill GO train station to Union Station (at the southern end of both north-south subway lines). To get to the Rouge Hill GO train station, cross Sheppard Avenue and take the Sheppard East 85A or 85D south. Before heading out on the trail, call GO Transit information at (416) 665-0022 for current bus and train schedules.

13. Scarborough Bluffs

2.5 miles/4 km

Towering 90 meters (300 feet) over the blue waters of Lake Ontario, the Scarborough Bluffs offer spectacular scenery. Bluffers Park, on reclaimed land jutting into Lake Ontario below the Bluffs, has walking, cycling and running. There is also walking along the driftwood-strewn sand beaches along the base of the Bluffs east of the park.

Carved over thousands of years by the pounding waves of Lake Ontario and eroded by winter frosts and spring rains, the Scarborough Bluffs record five glacial ages, demarcated by the layers of sand that at one time were the floors of pre-historic lakes. The oldest goes back one and a half billion years to the Precambrian Age, the period when the Canadian Shield that covers northern Ontario and much of northern Canada was formed.

Scarborough was named by Mrs. Elizabeth Simcoe, wife of Lieutenant Governor John Simcoe, because the Bluffs here resembled the cliffs at the North Sea resort of Scarborough, Yorkshire, about which the well-known centuries-old British folk-song "Are You Going to Scarborough Fair?" was written.

PUBLIC TRANSIT: Go to Warden subway station (on the Bloor-Danforth line), and take the Markham 102 or Bellamy 9 bus to the corner of St. Clair Avenue East and Brimley Road. Go right on Brimley Road. Walk south, past the "Welcome to Bluffers Park, Waterfront Park Systems" sign and down the hill to the park.

AUTOMOBILE: Get on Kingston Road, which is Highway 2, and go south on Brimley Road all the way down the hill to Bluffers Park and the parking lots.

THE WALK: When you reach the bottom of the hill, go to your right, past the washrooms and walk along the shore of the park. Go along the small coves and ponds. Here you can see Canada geese, ducks and other waterfowl. When you reach the eastern edge of the park, you can continue hiking on the driftwood-covered sandy beach at the base of the Bluffs. Walk and explore this wild area and then return to the park road.

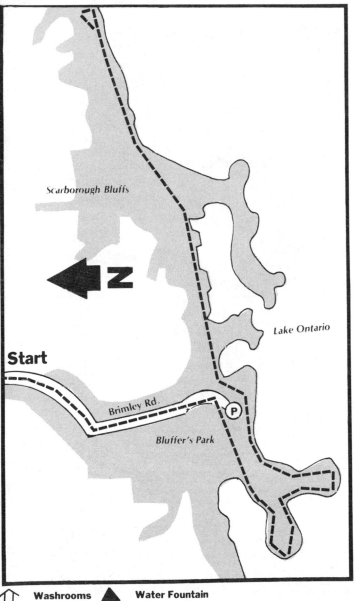

Start

Scarborough Bluffs

N

Lake Ontario

Brimley Rd.

P

Bluffer's Park

⇪ **Washrooms** ▲ **Water Fountain**

14. The Beaches

3.2 km/2 miles

A wooden boardwalk beside sandy beaches on Lake Ontario offers picturesque walking and running. A separate bicycling path is also provided.

One of the most popular walks in Toronto, the Beaches boardwalk is often full of walkers, baby carriages and dogs. Though not as wild as the ravines, the Beaches boardwalk offers a beautiful view of Lake Ontario. Seagulls and ducks are in abundance. During the evenings you can watch the lights of Great Lake freighters blink in the twilight. During a hot summer's day, the Beaches are covered with picnickers and sunbathers.

PUBLIC TRANSIT: There are several ways of reaching the Beaches. You can take the Queen Street East 501 streetcar from Queen subway station (on the Yonge Street line), east to any stop between Greenwood racetrack and Balsam Avenue, and walk south down to the lake.

Three Bloor-Danforth line subway stations also provide access to the Beaches. From Coxwell station, take the Coxwell 22 bus to Queen Street East. From Woodbine station, take the Woodbine South 92 bus to Queen Street East. From Main station take the Main 64 bus south to Queen Street East. From Queen Street East, it's a short walk south to Lake Ontario and the Beaches boardwalk.

AUTOMOBILE: Take the Lake Shore Boulevard East and turn off at the entrance to Ashbridges Bay Park and Woodbine Beach (opposite Coxwell Avenue) and follow the signs to the parking lots.

THE WALK: The Beaches boardwalk is accessible from many points. The easternmost part, along a section known as Balmy Beach, begins at Silver Birch Avenue just west of the water filtration plant. This part of the walk is bordered by large oak trees until Wineva Avenue. West of Wineva Avenue, the boardwalk goes along Kew Gardens which has baseball diamonds and paddle ball courts. At the base of Woodbine Avenue is the Beaches Olympic Pool. West of the pool, the boardwalk curves around the bay onto Ashbridges Bay Park, a grassy peninsula that juts into Lake Ontario. The boardwalk ends at the tip of the peninsula where there are benches and shelters from sun and rain.

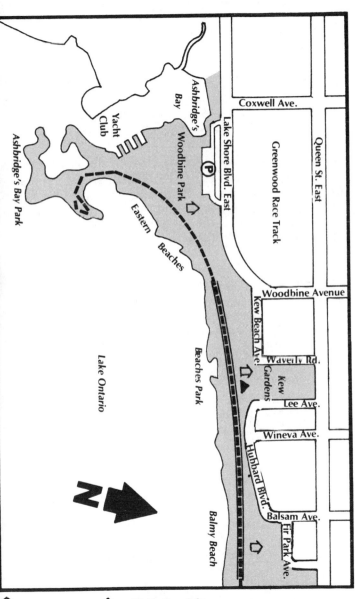

⇧ = **Washrooms** ▲ = **Water Fountain**

THE GREAT TORONTO BICYCLING GUIDE

The essential up-to-date handbook on enjoying cycling, THE GREAT TORONTO BICYCLING GUIDE traces 12 unique off-street bicycle paths in Metro Toronto. Each route description tells you how to reach the path by bicycle, car or subway and has an easy-to-read map as well as information on history and wildlife.

80 pages (Published by Great North Books) $3.95

THE COMPLETE GUIDE TO BICYCLING IN CANADA

Pick up this book and explore its over one hundred bicycle touring routes for a day, weekend, week, month or longer across Canada. THE COMPLETE GUIDE TO BICYCLING IN CANADA tells you how to get ready and guides you along each route with information on roads distances, attractions, weather, camping and accommodation.

400 pages (Published by Doubleday) $19.95

THE COMPLETE GUIDE TO WALKING IN CANADA

For walkers and hikers! THE COMPLETE GUIDE TO WALKING IN CANADA is the only book that covers the vast resources Canada's natural areas offer you. Details on the topography, climate, wildlife, the length of walks, hikes and backpacking treks in every province and territory, as well as sections on hiking with children, finding your way, equipment, insects and winter are included.

288 pages (Published by Doubleday) $14.95

GREAT COUNTRY WALKS AROUND TORONTO

Let friends and family enjoy Toronto's most scenic country walking trails. Order additional copies for every occasion.

64 pages (Published by Great North Books) $3.95

Available at your favourite bookseller or direct by mail.
Order from: Great North Books
60 Bayhampton Crescent
Thornhill, Ontario L4J 7G9